DEER

Published by Smart Apple Media
1980 Lookout Drive, North Mankato, Minnesota 56003

Design and Production by The Design Lab/Kathy Petelinsek

Photographs by Premiere Stock & Fine Art.
Additional photographs by Tom Stack & Associates (2, 3, 22)

Library of Congress Cataloging-in-Publication Data
Frisch, Aaron.
Deer / by Aaron Frisch
p. cm. – (Northern Trek)
Includes resources, glossary, and index
Summary: Describes the behavior, habitat, physical characteristics, and hunting and
conservation of deer, specifically mule deer.
ISBN 1-58340-036-2
1. Mule deer–Juvenile literature. [1. Mule deer. 2. Deer.] I. Title. II. Series: Northern Trek (Mankato, Minn.)

QL737.U55F75   2000
599.65'3–dc21   99-053536

First Edition

2   4   6   8   9   7   5   3   1

DEER

WRITTEN BY AARON FRISCH
PHOTOGRAPHS BY PREMIERE STOCK & FINE ART

SMART APPLE MEDIA

Much of the western half of North America is rugged land. This area includes the Rocky Mountains, the Badlands of North and South Dakota, and the rolling hills in between. Spread across this uneven landscape are millions of mule deer, one of the most common species of deer on the continent. With antlers resembling tree branches and long ears like a mule's, mule deer are as majestic-looking as the land they call home. More of these animals are alive today than perhaps at any other time in history.

MALE MULE DEER

(*Odocoileus hemionus*), called bucks, stand about three and a half feet (1.07 m) tall at the shoulder. They usually weigh close to 200 pounds (91 kg), though they can grow to twice that weight. Females, called does, are a little shorter and usually weigh about 150 pounds (68 kg). The mule deer's reddish coat turns gray or brown just before winter.

Bucks grow large, impressive antler racks. The **antlers** start to grow in the spring. Throughout the summer, they can grow as much as three inch-

es (7.5 cm) per week. During this time, they are covered by velvet, a soft tissue that helps carry blood to the growing antlers. By September, the antlers are finished growing for the year, and the velvet slowly falls off as they harden. The bucks use their fully-developed antlers to fight other bucks during the **breeding season**. Then, in the middle of winter, their antlers fall off.

Female mule deer and their young travel together in small groups. During the summer, they feed on grass high in the hills.

When spring comes, mule deer start growing new antlers again. Every year, the antlers get a little bigger until the buck is four or five years old. At that age, the buck is in his **prime** and his antlers are as big as they will get. Each full-grown antler may have four to six branches, called points.

Mule deer live across most of the western half of North America, from northern Mexico to southern parts of Alaska. They are hardy animals that can survive in many different kinds of **habitat**, including deserts, plains, and forests. Most mule deer, however, choose to live in hilly or mountainous areas, where they can easily hide and spot **predators** from a long distance.

A mule deer's antlers grow fastest early in the summer, when there are a lot of nutritious plants available for the deer to eat.

Fully-grown mule deer antlers may measure 32 inches (81 cm) across at the tips. Bucks use their antlers to fight other bucks, to chase away enemies, and to dig for food.

Because they live in various habitats, mule deer eat many kinds of vegetation. Their food includes grass, mushrooms, nuts, berries, and the leaves and twigs of small trees. Mule deer feed at sunrise and sunset. After a deer finishes eating its meal—usually about 10 pounds (4.5 kg) of food—it lays down to rest. Mule deer normally rest in open feeding areas at night and in hills or thick brush during the day. They get most of the water they need just from the moisture in plants.

In the winter, mule deer usually live in valleys, where it is warmer and easier to dig through the snow for food.

Mule deer bucks fight furiously to win mates. They lock their massive antler racks together, then use their strong back legs to drive opponents backward or down to the ground.

Mule deer bucks live alone for most of the year, while the does and their young live together in small groups. Late in the fall, though, bucks start to look for does. During this time—the breeding season—bucks mark their **territories** by rubbing their **scent** on tree branches. If other males move into the area to mate with the same females, two bucks will fight by locking their antlers together and having a pushing match. Only the strongest bucks usually win mates.

About seven months after the breeding season, does give birth to one, two, or three fawns. The fawns weigh three to eight pounds (1.5-3.5 kg) at birth and are covered with beautiful spots that help them blend in with their surroundings. For the first month, before they can run fast, fawns spend most of their time hiding from predators in tall grass. The young deer usually stay with their mothers until they are one or two years old. Although mule deer in zoos may live 20 years, most deer in the wild live less than 10.

Besides human hunters, a mule deer's main enemies are wolves, coyotes, and mountain lions. Mule deer can see, smell, and hear well, which makes them very good at detecting predators. If a mule deer senses something unusual nearby, it will walk slowly toward it, stomping its feet. This may be either to warn other deer or to try to scare any enemies away.

Mule deer are born with reddish coats and spots. By their first winter, though, young deer have solid-colored coats.

Mule deer have unusual methods of escaping predators. Keeping their legs very stiff, they hop on all four legs at once, bounding away like jackrabbits. This strange running style allows the deer to see their surroundings clearly and helps them to move quickly over uneven ground. The mule deer's powerful legs—which make it a good swimmer as well—allow it to hit running speeds of up to 40 miles (64 km) per hour over short distances.

When chased by predators, mule deer choose the most rugged escape route possible. By bounding over logs, bushes, and boulders, mule deer create a kind of obstacle course for the predator following them. Mule deer often stop to look

Mule deer like to live as far from humans as possible. They are strong and hardy animals that can tolerate both hot and cold conditions equally well.

When alarmed, mule deer make short whistling noises through their nose. They also communicate with each other using snorting, barking, and bleating sounds.

back at the enemy while escaping. This seems to help them plan where to run to next.

Mule deer have been hunted by humans for centuries. Native Americans ate mule deer **venison** and made deer skins into a fine kind of leather called buckskin. When European colonists arrived in America, they killed so many mule deer that the species was wiped out from most of its range in eastern North America. By 1900, the only mule deer left lived west of the Mississippi River.

Strangely, more mule deer exist in the United States today than when the first settlers came to America. There are two main reasons for this population increase. First, many forests were gradually cut down by loggers. Although this was bad for many kinds of animals, it helped the mule

deer by creating clearings where more food could grow. Second, hunters killed almost all of the wolves and mountain lions by the early 1900s, so the mule deer had fewer enemies.

Because of its spectacular antlers and excellent meat, hunters today still consider the mule deer one of the most prized game animals in North America. Although hunters kill about 500,000 mule deer every year, the wild population is safe and well-managed. Wildlife experts estimate that more than five million of these stunning animals continue to roam North America.

Mule deer are most active around sunrise and sunset, when they move into open areas to feed. They can see well in the dark and have excellent hearing, which helps them to avoid enemies that hunt at night.

MULE DEER ARE COMMON

across much of the western United States and Canada, but they can best be viewed in parks and refuges that protect their habitat. Because mule deer feed at sunrise and sunset, these are the best times to catch them moving about. You may also spot them resting in open feeding areas at the end of the day. Listed below are some mule deer habitats with public access. As with any trek into nature, it is important to remember that wild animals are unpredictable and can be dangerous if approached. The best way to view wildlife is from a respectful—and safe—distance.

THE GREAT BASIN REGION *This area of the western United States includes Bear River Migratory Bird Refuge in Brigham City, Utah; the Malheur National Wildlife Refuge in Burns, Oregon; and the Great Basin National Park in Baker, Nevada.*

NORTHERN ROCKY MOUNTAINS *The northern region of this mountain range includes many parks and forests with good public access to mule deer habitats. Some are Glacier National Park, in Montana, and Canada's very first national park, Banff, in Alberta. Idaho's Nez Perce, Clearwater, and Coeur d'Alene National Forests and Montana's Lolo, Gallatin, and Flathead National Forests are also included in this region.*

THE GREAT PLAINS *This vast region, extending from Texas to Canada, includes the Little Missouri, Thunder Basin, Cimarron, and Black Kettle National Grasslands, as well as Theodore Roosevelt and Badlands National Parks. Mule deer populations are high throughout much of this region.*

antlers: *the hard growths on some kinds of hoofed animals used for defense and browsing for food*

breeding season: *a time when male and female animals come together to mate*

habitat: *a place where a plant or animal normally lives*

predators: *animals that kill other animals for food*

prime: *the time of an animal's life when it is strongest and most active*

scent: *an odor left by an animal on a tree or other marker*

territories: *specific areas where animals sleep and eat*

venison: *deer meat*